Rapture & the Big Bam

Snowbound Chapbook Award, Previous Winners

Barbara Tran, *In the Mynah Bird's Own Words*
Selected by Robert Wrigley

David Hernandez, *A House Waiting for Music*
Selected by Ray Gonzalez

Mark Yakich, *The Making of Collateral Beauty*
Selected by Mary Ruefle

Joy Katz, *The Garden Room*
Selected by Lisa Russ Spaar

Cecilia Woloch, *Narcissus*
Selected by Marie Howe

John Cross, *staring at the animal*
Selected by Gillian Conoley

Stacey Waite, *the lake has no saint*
Selected by Dana Levin

Brandon Som, *Babel's Moon*
Selected by Aimee Nezhukumatathil

Kathleen Jesme, *Meridian*
Selected by Patricia Fargnoli

Anna George Meek, *Engraved*
Selected by Ellen Doré Watson

Deborah Flanagan, *Or, Gone*
Selected by Christopher Buckley

Chad Parmenter, *Weston's Unsent Letters to Modotti*
Selected by Kathleen Jesme

Allan Peterson, *Other Than They Seem*
Selected by Ruth Ellen Kocher

Rapture & the Big Bam

Matt Donovan

TUPELO PRESS
North Adams, Massachusetts

Rapture and teh Big Bam.
Copyright © 2017 Matt Donovan. All rights reserved.

ISBN: 978-1-936797-94-3

Cover and text designed by Howard Klein.
Back cover photograph: "Delivered, San Francisco, 2010," by Kate Joyce. Copyright © 2010 Kate Joyce (www.kate-joyce.com). Used with permission.

First edition: March 2017.

Other than brief excerpts for reviews and commentaries, no part of this book may be reproduced by any means without permission of the publisher. Please address requests for reprint permission or for course-adoption discounts to:

Tupelo Press
P.O. Box 1767, North Adams, Massachusetts 01247
Telephone: (413) 664–9611 / editor@tupelopress.org / www.tupelopress.org

Tupelo Press is an award-winning independent literary press that publishes fine fiction, nonfiction, and poetry in books that are a joy to hold as well as read. Tupelo Press is a registered 501(c)(3) nonprofit organization, and we rely on public support to carry out our mission of publishing extraordinary work that may be outside the realm of the large commercial publishers. Financial donations are welcome and are tax deductible.

for Cyrus & for Oliver

Contents

3	Still Life with Burnt Lake
5	Exit, Pursued by a Bear
7	Bessie Smith's Last Recorded Song
9	Prelude for Musical Glasses
11	Rapture & the Big Bam
13	Elegy with Mistakes All Through It
16	Poem in which Billie Holiday Is Barely Heard
18	Motel Makeshift Lullaby
20	How to Paint the Sea
23	Two Songs About the Work of Hands
25	"Perhaps We Are What We Want to Remember"
27	Sargent Adrift at the Trenches
30	To No One
32	Van Gogh's First Sunday Sermon

~

37	Notes
38	Acknowledgments

Rapture & the Big Bam

Still Life with Burnt Lake

In Burnet's *Sacred Theory of the Earth,* our pre-Fall,
heaven-girding world is a smooth, featureless orb
& nothing mars the flawless globe — not the dying
sycamore with its papery hives, not the soda-sticky
steps the mall skaters topple down one by one.
But in order to imagine this unimaginable earth
forever circling his mind, he's forced to rummage
our lapsed world: *egg-smooth,* he wrote, *like river stones.*
Like a ripening melon. Or,
                                 if I had to guess, something
like a resplendent Cezanne plum that seems less
about actual fruit than form & chromatic smears:
oxheart, cobalt, peach black. A story: a woman I knew
long ago told me the day she chose to cut into her skin
& become the shell she wanted to be, she was saved
by an orange rind someone propped on a fence post
then reassembled as a nearly round scrap. *There it was,*
she told me, but otherwise couldn't
                                 say much about this
frost-shriveled trash peeled into a single frayed strip.
Bright ochre bangles inscribing spider legs, indigo
blaze of a button — there might be, within any of this,
the seed of some theory on longing, but what good
to unpack any balm not my own? And yet, here I am
scouring late Cezanne, still lifes painted so slowly
he used wax fruit & fake blossoms to stave off decay.
I work with difficulty, but in the end,
                      there is something
he writes, as if wary of any creed beyond the vague
husks of words, and perhaps meaning nothing more

than persimmons on a zinc white plate, lustrous
globed heaps of cherries. Which doesn't stop me
from guessing at his last letter, a few peevish words
whipped off to a paint merchant even as he starts to die:
It's been eight days since I asked you for ten burnt lakes —
denial? solace in grappling after anything that remains?
mere scrawl lifted from elegy into that hoped-for flare
of red? — *and I have received no reply. What is the matter?*
Pneumonia will take him a day from now, & yet he awakes
at dawn & begins, beneath a lime tree's shade, a portrait
of his gardener. *An answer, and a quick one, I beg you.*

Exit, Pursued by a Bear

Given the flecks of October stars, the withered scribble
of garden shapes, I sit listening hard to the night as if
there were nothing else to do. A bit of wind & that

on-the-prowl screech-yip of coyotes, something snuffling
the oaks again. Must we love this? Yet another autumn
tramping it down, all the meager stuff we blunder toward,

hoard for consolation, how each day lurches us toward —
as *The Winter's Tale* has it — things dying, things newborn.
If that play is true, someone once began, though I can't imagine

how he finished the thought. Small hope, in any case,
since it's all a fabulous lie: that concocted Bohemian coast,
the long-dead resurrected as statue, stepping down

stage-right and Antigonus eaten by that matter-of-fact bear
after he abandons the child. No one can explain how,
in the months before my son was born, it seemed there was

a funeral every week. Believe me: since I can't say anything
that seems true about either the dying or newborn, I wish
the detritus from that time might somehow be worth more:

stacks of creamers on red-eye flights, another thick-striped tie.
Or deep within a room that seemed to be lumbering away,
where no one spoke of morphine drips or cancer consuming

a face, a third cousin describing the sky opening in sorrow
after a Longhorn loss. The skies open as Antigonus is mauled
off-stage & the storm swallows a boatload of men

like raisins in flaming brandy — that it's all untrue brings
no one back & between the sea, the wind, the bear & the man,
there's too much roaring to speak of, although a shepherd tries.

He tries even as the howling reaches its pitch, yet exits
whooping of luck since by then he's found the impossible
girl with her basket of gold. Meaning even if there's more

to say about devouring, leave room for blessing, grace.
Thus lying in bed, black clothes crimped on chair-backs
for the next unending day, pressing the rim of a glass

into the unlikely globe of my wife's eight-month belly,
inscribing fast-fading ring upon ring & hearing nothing
of course but at least knowing what I was listening for.

Bessie Smith's Last Recorded Song

As if in the wide space of nothing she leaves between *lovin'*

& *whole* there might be some kind of hint. But she couldn't

give two fried shits for what you know about her end,

discography, the blank gaze of taillights on some empty road.

Listen, & you won't hear what will be not long from now —

smack dab in the boil of another lurching grind, why think

this is it? On *Down in the Dumps* with Buck & his Band,

she's worlds away from any Mississippi two-lane stretch,

let alone wailing for coins outside a Chattanooga saloon,

from hum-along filler on wax-papered combs, or Hack Back,

the Ukulele Wonder, noodling his way through boilerplate tunes

& the crooked constellation of sequins spelling *Sassy*

down her faux-velvet back. *Gimmie a pigfoot*

& a bottle of beer she's just growled into the sour mouth

of a horn, but as the master disc spins in midtown,

her voice engraved into grooves, she's long sashayed

from that too. From her canned shtick on pared-down sets

where the spotlight stood in as a ramshackle moon,

or from the moon gauzing that magnolia grove where —

you can't help but circle back — a man has stopped

his bread truck again, worried his wheels might burst.

He leans back against the hood, feeling the day's heat

still crouched on the road, hearing the night brim

with bullfrog, cicada, his engine's click & whirr. Flit of wind

through ditch thorns, slosh of what's left in his jug. Even though

soon Bessie's car will sideswipe him grumbling into gear

& topple with its axle sheared off, he knows, as she does

bellowing out this song, that he's broad strides away

from anything happening except for the grip of this *now*.

Prelude for Musical Glasses

    Something like Melville's honey hunter leaning in too far,
dying encased in sweetness. Yet without the elegiac whiff.
    Or those songs of Orpheus before the glance back,
when his lyre's strummed guts still made the brambles sag

    with oozy berries & made rivers buck from silt-churning paths
where wild beasts lolled glassy-eyed, inhaling the sugary tunes
    about a bite of tongue-spun apple in Eurydice's mouth
& not much else beyond the sputtering torches & gilded things

    he knew would adorn his wedding day, which would be soon.
Such were the heavenly sounds Ben Franklin made
    as his fingertips, ever-wet with the rainwater they grazed,
skimmed soda-lime bowls rigged to turn on an iron rod

    & the rims gave off a ravishing, high-pitched keen that swelled
into the indescribable, never-needing-to-be-tuned sublime.
    Or at least this is more or less how, during the short-lived
glass harp craze, its notes were described as *perfect*. Armonica,

    Franklin called it, from the Italian for *harmony*, & for all
his doohickey dabbling — soothing wind-pummeled waves
    with tumblers of oil, that iconic kite lashed by blustering skies —
nothing made him giddier than this contraption he built

    in order to have the unworldly music of angels at the whim
of nearly motionless hands. An instrument he played shuttered tight
    in his cobalt third-floor room, keeping the sun's blare
from each damp spinning glass, the same way he taught

Marie Antoinette in the velvet-curtained parlors of Versailles
as she stood bejeweled in her diamond-dusted two-foot pouf,
   fingering crystal goblets for the gathered palace crowd
obliged to think of nothing but the tremulous aria she made.

   For hours they listened, pretending it was all that mattered,
& at times it almost was, as if each piercing note were prelude
   to nothing, severed from any thought of what's to come.
The way, the first time her husband plays, Franklin's wife,

   dragged up from a sheet-thrashing sleep, sits rapt
watching dust motes pour down into a tiny square of light,
   knowing for a moment she's dead. As motionless as
you in a heat-haze at the pier, clutching what's left

   of your fist-warmed coins, listening to a man cram the air
with ethereal noise that is the theme to *Popeye* & might be
   the worst thing ever made. His hands flutter — emphatic,
precise — above the gleaming rows of glass & where do you go

   from this empty rapture, stock still, dazzled despite it all?

Rapture & the Big Bam

Transported by trifles these soupy days — bright-blooming
paprika yarrow, that bagpiped out-of-tune *Auld Lang Syne*
tumbling over bone-dry hills, my son trembling with bliss

& dread as he topples down the frog-slide's tongue —
I grow wary of my own whirligig bouts of delight
when I find myself sideswiped by a ball of electrical tape

made, the plaque claims, *by Babe Ruth at St. Mary's School for Boys.*
Needless to say, who cares? Why pause for even a moment
before this misshapen tchotchke on a Plexiglas shelf? Relic-like,

under a hard light's glare, beside Cobb's sharpened cleats
& Clemente's jersey from such & such a game, it was a wad
of nothing, really, a lopsided sphere most likely never used

for a game or even shagging flies & is only one more piece
of the past's lumpish fruit turned artifact behind alarmed glass.
And still, why pretend the wondrous & the useless weren't the same

all along? The meaningless, the miraculous — who are we to say?
Picture this tight bundle sailing past each backpedaling boy
history swallowed whole, long past the orphanage wall-notch

marking Brother Mathias's furthest shot, past that rusted boiler
& the harbor's rotting hulls, & past now even what legend will allow
as it soars beyond his Pigtown two-room shack with its avalanche

of bottles & chairs & his sauced-up father lurking again, back
from a day of door-to-door lies about his worthless lightning rods,
flames, guarantees, God's wrath. Or at least this is how

it might have seemed. Rapture, *raptura: to carry away
with joy*; earlier: *to kidnap, rape*, although for better or worse
in this simmer of pleasure no one's talking etymology here.

In the last year Ruth played for the Sox, he pummeled
a slider off Columbia George for the longest homerun ever hit.
With ease. Without much of anything but a body-thrashing stroke

during spring training when, as if it were possible, all of this
means even less. Billy Sunday, ex-right-fielder-turned-preacher-ablaze,
taking a break from bellowing about the Devil's spitballs

& ways to head-butt sin, watched that ball beeline for even more
empty sky & for as long as this fast-winging shape remains
aloft, & even for a bit longer still, it's the only grace

Sunday or anyone could feel, buoying them beyond the far wall
& revival tent pitched across the field, the bay's abandoned shipyards,
all the dead that year from flu. Or is this too much to presume?

Even if perfection here means a split-second thwack & all
the countless ways to be held in thrall are both our shame & luck,
it matters little just now. I tell you no one could help their joy.

Elegy with Mistakes All Through It

How the crash took weeks of planning — a dwarfing
Ringling Brothers wind-snared tent, the soon-to-be-junked
engines painted with lime-green trim, miles of track
veering from the main Katy line & freshly dug wells
for the tens of thousands who watched The Crush Collision,
an arranged wreck to scrap two trains already doomed
in order to make a buck. The way the whistle-locked
engines plunged the track, howling for nothing before
pummeling head-on, & when the boilers ruptured,
shrapnel pelted down like rain & even though a few
were killed in the stampede, the crowd sprinted back
to the still-hot metal, prying up souvenirs. Scott Joplin,
we think, also looked on, concocting a song in aftermath,
no matter the distance between the piano's syncopated clack
& that still-steaming ruin. This is guesswork, of course —
nearly all the traces of Joplin's roundabout path turned
long ago to char. Which didn't stop my grappling after
those empty scraps as you played for me that last time.
How long before I wandered off into my scattered thoughts
about an earth-trembling roar Joplin maybe heard, or how
in a smoke-clogged brothel on Battle Row, the pasties
on a girl named Bubbie grazed the man's neck as he burned
through the refrain? I want that day back. To listen again
to the soft-shoe rhythms you found in the backbeat
of Joplin & Bach, to hear you work even a few notes
of those partitas & rags which consumed your last years.
Was it even the *Crush Collision March* you played?
I heard *Bethena*, I think, a near-dirge written just after
his second wife died a few weeks past their wedding,
although some think that song trawls another loss

altogether. To be honest, I can't remember much
except the wind & your walker's scrape as you limped
to the bench which would be, I know, the last thing
you'd want me to say. Let me try again. *This piece,
this piece*, you once began, beaming, clutching
the B Minor Mass score to your chest before drifting
into silence, as if everything you meant was clear.
Making me — fourteen, gangly, acne-pocked, slumped
at the keys — insist all the more that the jangle-slurred
chords of *Sweet Jane* could kick the ass of any chorus.
What did I know? *Precisely jackshit*, you made it clear,
especially about Bach, who had twenty kids, you told me
during my first lesson, *so you know he loved fucking*.
Which didn't stop me griping each week about trills,
finely wrought fugues, the harpsichord's frail plucking.
Or, later, the leapfrogging left hand of *'S Wonderful*
I botched until you slammed the keyboard shut & asked,
*Kid, why do you waste my time? Any chance it's because
I'm black?* Who knows what I stammered back, sweating
in silence, October light pooling the room? Or why
you humored me all those years, even as I butchered
scale after scale & my still-cracking voice hacked up
the Halleluiah Chorus before you ordered me
to *just mouth every goddamn word. Please.* It was easy
enough to move my lips, following along, pretending
to exalt the stretched-to-breaking syllables of *forever*,
a word repeated & made slack until it seemed to collapse,
meaning it began to mean again. *Ragtime*, Joplin said,
because the time is ragged. Old friend, might it be
more so. Might time break from its metronome tick
that carries me further from the days you were here,
from the wind's caterwaul & the cloud-muddled sky
that last time I half-heard you play. *Without music,*

I'd die, you once told me matter of fact, & for a time
we both pretended the correlate was true: you'd live
as long as there was song. Why can't there be one thing
that seems enough just now? Watch how my monkey-mind
leaves melody behind for a riff on John Taylor, eye-surgeon,
chevalier, a Don Juan who blinded both Handel & Bach
with his straying incisions & useless hodgepodge
of balms made from pigeon blood, sugar, baked salt.
What am I doing, now that you're gone, starting this piece
with a train wreck, or any disaster held at arm's length?
If all I'm trying to say, while bounding through pimples,
Gershwin, Lou Reed, is something we already know
about failure & grief, just how far am I from Taylor
the Quack's smoke-&-mirror cures, his trademark carriage
covered with blind, wide-open, embroidered eyes
wild-gawking in every direction? Do you remember
once, out of nowhere, stopping the class & making us
listen to Coltrane's *Alabama*? No one said a thing
as the words from the eulogy for the four girls bombed
in the Birmingham church were translated into breath
driven through tenor sax & we heard that lament
unfastened from threadbare words, prayer turned wholly
to song. *Are you shitting me*, I can almost hear you say,
what are you doing, using that as a bridge, a means?
Forgive me, as always, my bungling. My false starts
& how the loss of you trumps all other loss today.
All I mean to evoke is language becoming
a disconsolate wail. Unearthly, resolute. Or
even the single note McCoy Tyner plays chant-like
for nearly that entire song, hammering the same key
as if unable to stop, or knowing it was the sole thing
sufficient. *Enough, enough*, I know you'd say. *Stop.*
For fuck's sake. Listen.

Poem in which Billie Holiday Is Barely Heard

    Her voice a velvet backdrop
to mood-thirsty sex or scrubbing
        bathroom tiles. A giddy *All of Me*
    gives way to *Strange Fruit* which turns

    to gauze I partly ignore
over chorizo-stuffed quail, little spoons
        teeming with sorbet, talk of wax-jobs,
    committee snafus. For all I ever hear,

    her songs might as well be the spatter
of meat in a pan as Holiday smirks
        in her apron, searing the meal,
    not wanting just then to offer up

    anything but this fried steak for her dog,
Mister, who must be gagging for it
        yet in the photo isn't letting on
    & gazes, saint-like, straight ahead.

    No one, she bragged, sang *hunger* like her,
although one night it was the plunging
        tail end vibrato of *forevermore*
    which cleaved a party's drone

    before it was lost to the humdrum
clarinet solo & whatever I went on to say.
        I've ransacked song after song
    looking for those notes — they're gone,

  vanished the way she did at the end
of her set, lights cued to cut out
    on the last beat, letting her stream
  offstage in darkness back to her room

  for a fix. Another shot: glamour gladiolas,
clusters of pearls, spotlight snaring
    that hokey, ceramic angel
  someone nailed up above the stage

  & her lips locked on a shard
of melody as her hands hover,
    palms up, the lie so beautiful
  we forget it's luck that nothing lasts.

  Her voice trails off, frayed, out of tune;
Mister laps up gin at the White Rose,
    then is mauled by Basie's Pekinese —
  yet more songs we're still learning to hear

  about our tumbled grace as grace.
Towards the end, at Carnegie Hall,
    she trips onstage just before
  the band vamps her opening tune

  six times through as she clutches
the mike, too weak to stand,
    her body a constellation of scars.
  What is this? she asks, baffled

  by the chords, the melody dissolved,
& it seemed as if it would last forever
    until they heard her say *Ah, Blue Moon!*
  & everyone began breathing.

Motel Makeshift Lullaby

When you scream again from the towel-padded drawer, I'm awake already,
listening to the snow-squall & semis leaning into night, to Lee Marvin
muttering one-liners next door, someone slurring *Baby, I need some ice.*

For an hour, I've heard you too, thrashing in your makeshift crib
just to feel, I think, your body move until you become inconsolable again.
Two counties from here, in Spillville, Dvorak once summered

with cold ale & Czechs, roosting in wild clover & cornflower seas,
in swelter crammed with joy, even when storms bellowed down
&, panicked, he'd batter the piano with whatever scherzo-like thing

seized his mind, trying to drown out what was coming, what was
fiercely already there. Little one, forget Dvorak's thunder. Forget
this storm too, which thrashed us from the road & stalls us here.

You've eaten but wail on, gripped by hunger of another kind. All I meant
to summon up in this menthol-stale room was a simple gladness:
steaming ocher mug, a smaller, swaddled you, both of us watching

rust-backed birds in thin dawn light scatter the clamoring finches,
& then watching what looked like blossoms spilling impossibly
from between two bricks until it became what it was: a hatch

of winged ants rising in waves, spiraling petal-like into sky.
Crossing the Iowa prairies, Dvorak found in the waving grasses,
in the sway & whorl of foxtail that let loose a rasping he loved,

sorrow he never explained. Or that he explains in his Dumky trio,
a piece shaped by Hungarian poems in which the melancholy must end
as a manic dance. Tonight, miles from any place I might want to be,

thinking of nights you'll inherit, I clasp you tight, balloon you
through this mostly-dark, hobble to the music locked in my head
that is not some magisterial adagio, but the tune of staccato babble

that gave you earlier today a fluky shriek of joy: Boogie Boy Perkins's
tenor-wild *Ba Da.* Why not? *Dumka, Dvorak*: any clump of sounds will do.
Ba Da tonight is your cradlesong, & what I whisper down to your head,

to your mother now tumbling back into sleep, into the smoke-stained
wallpaper of roses that twist into violets, weave back to roses again,
to our room's tiny soap, to the ice-less couple next door. Song-of-want,

for all it's worth, to your song-of-want — small dervish within this storm.

How to Paint the Sea

    Try strapping yourself like Turner to the mast, hurling
pell-mell straight into the storm, squinting through rain-slash
        & salt-soaked air, dissecting the whipped, unfathomable

wave-frenzied howl as if he owned all the tumbling seas,
        knowing terror will translate to palette then brush, sure
he'll nail it as it was. Or at least the way he wants it to seem,

    rollicked with impasto, glistening bitumen, smears
of ochre walnut-oiled & whatever form demands, the paint
        poured, stroked, hand-smudged, corralled to give back

the wilderness he saw Ulysses-like lashed with ropes.
        Or not at all, given his love of apocrypha, given how
his story of rendering this storm seems filched from Homer's

    sirens crooning desire, beckoning across the sea
in what, poor word, we call *song*. In that version,
        though, once the ship has sailed on from melodies

& beach-washed bones, the island's yellow crocus spilling
        in waves, no one asks about the indescribable sounds
& the poem veers from the hero as he must have been:

    slouched near the helm in silence, unfurled, inconsolable,
ravished still. What words could he have used? Ruskin writes
        Turner's painting of Ulysses mocking the Cyclops is as perfect

as human work can be, but if you muttered *scumbled clouds,*
    vaulted sky above burnished waves, wouldn't you still be
a long journey off from that exact sunrise, split-wide, swelling,

    the museum's flat light blotting the prow? In its grandeur
crammed on the postcard you hold, you can't even discern
    what you're told you should see: Apollo buried within

the horizon's butterscotch & flecks of plum that somehow
    add up to light he hauls, whip-cracking his chariot's horses,
or even the Cyclops, cliff-side, the art books insist, howling

    with rage, hurling boulders at the man who escaped back
to the ocean's wide arms by clinging to the belly of a sheep.
    You consider the greasy tufts of wool, that thunderous rain

of stones, the breeze-flung pine outside, the nimble flick
    of the mailman's hand as he delivers what you'll throw away
& purrs off through a darkening afternoon, humming

    some Sinatra you can almost place & weigh it all
against each swift-footed god, the olive-shaded courtyard
    where the suitors' bodies are stacked & the maids lynched

like thrushes on a wire, Homer tells us, then thinks again:
    no, more like pigeons, thrashing wild-winged in a thicket.
None of this now seems at all about the sea, & you're still

    far from where you'd like to be, as Ulysses is too,
unmoored after his homecoming, forced to travel inland
    with an oar on his back to wage peace with the god

of untamable water. He must walk until he finds someone
    who has never heard of waves or ships & confuses
his oar with a winnowing fan & make his sacrifices there.

    Admit you too know nothing of the sea & watch now
the slaughter's heavy work, a blackened ram's horn
    licked by flames. Your dumb luck is to stand in error

before this charred bit of earth that tells you
    nothing, but seems as vast as something you know
you'll never name & out of this silence begin.

Two Songs About the Work of Hands

    Sawtooth daffodil streams. Beige angel strumming a harp.
The moon a clump of celluloid buttons tucked into
    a chenille sky. At first no surprise for the samplers

my neighbor gathered from her great-aunt's home
    now that the estate will be sold. Blocky heaps
of pineapples, a pointillist alphabet bordered with urns,

    linsey-woolsey peach-gray stags. *Born to Shop,*
intricate *Amens,* the curlicue *Our Father* they'd watched
    her hands flit across during potlucks & halftime lulls.

But behind her garage deep freezer, they found stacks
    of improbable others: the fashioned names
of phobias & ailments patterned, embellished, adorned.

    A rococo *Diabetes. Taphephobia* in a flourish
of serifs flanked with tulips & sheep. *Hypochondria.*
    Psoriasis. Five herringbone *Ulcers* — would it help

to insist this is true? — curving into a wreath.
    Robert Schumann, in Endenich, dying in the asylum,
most days pours over maps: the aqua-meandering of rivers,

    mountains in a crosshatch furze, Baltic shallows
clustered in thumbprints widening to the white of the sea.
    And the inked exactness of each name he plucks,

whispers, then writes in order on a page
    swelling with this daily work. *Berlin. Bonn. Borstel.*
Lübben. Lübeck. Luckau. He's making use, perhaps,

of the known world in the only way he still can —
listening to the music of syllables change. Or something
    else entirely. Hearing the silence between

each sayable thing & what he still can conjure
    of the actual place: chain of hawkweed on Clara's neck;
cantaloupe on bone-white plates. In a shore town once —

Cuxhaven? Emden? — a plunge bath's sudden grip.
How is this possible? my neighbor asks again,
    & touching the gauze of another one, she's right

not to know. Is it enough to say someone has formed,
    stitch by stitch, what she needed to inscribe: words
for what consumes her body & mind & the girding

    tokens of this world? Teeming baskets of apples & violets,
willows dwarfing a home; the careful calligraphy
    of *Sarcoma*, fear of waves, the heart. *My exquisite suffering,*

Schumann writes, after another night gazing at the ceiling
    as it burns, fissures, then becomes a porthole to heaven
blaring the same three notes again. When he wandered out

    to drown himself in the darkness of the Rhine,
he wavered at the toll gate in his slippers,
    then pressed into the guard's palm a handkerchief

which was all in that moment he had. Long after
    Schumann has been hauled ashore & the carnival mobs
have streamed past, the watchman stands alone

    in the rain — how else to imagine him? — holding
this useless, gaudy bit of silk with sudden awe & care,
    wondering where to put it, what to do with his hands.

"Perhaps We Are What We Want to Remember"

Take Saint Augustine at his word, & watch as you become

last May's cold snap crusting locust buds, one sticky night

tipped back in bucket seats, three neat rows of gravel

in a shoebox labeled *Petrified Rain*. Cleaved emerald shells

of a dragonfly snared in a wolf spider's web, that mouth

biscotti-crammed you can't ever give up. And what you're not,

since these are merely things which surface at times —

undesired, unbidden — is the doughy, swollen neck of some guy

named Barry at the Vatican who collapsed into your arms,

that tangerine-poached, gone-off tilapia choked down in bed,

or a gap-toothed Mac Magoon, freckled with cupcake, bat-wild

beneath a piñata as you touch Sarah Jordan's sun-burnt calf

beneath that leopard-print spread. *Memory*, Augustine wrote,

is like a great field, one in which leek-like hibiscus roots creep

through soil until, on an otherwise forgettable day, they flame with morning light in a bourbon-bottle vase. Or one in which

a farmer finds among his withered stalks an owl that he guesses

must have grazed the electrical wires, its talons still gripping

some sleek, whiskered creature. Although this is what you hear

mumbled from a diner's smoke-filled booth as you finger each name

carved into the tabletop, about now you should drop the act.

No one believes you want to become a cream-colored beak

in a dying patch of earth, that ant-rich feather splay.

Doesn't this dead bird engraved in someone else's mind

allow you to loosen the hold on your own chosen past,

those misremembered scraps of what you once held to your lips,

to your bare, pimply chest beneath the Ocean City boardwalk

as night surf tossed & churned? Admit you remain what you are:

a man eavesdropping at the Kettle Stop, someone wishing

what would last of today was something more than that electric-blue

smear of boysenberry syrup, someone else's story about wings.

Sargent Adrift at the Trenches

> The naked eye cannot catch it,
> nor have I, so far, forged the Vulcan's net in which the act can be imprisoned
> & looked gaily upon. How can there be anything flagrant enough for a picture
> when Mars & Venus are miles apart whether in camps or in the front trenches?
>
> — John Singer Sargent, 1918

God of the bellows & black clouds of making,
    cuckold, slow one, bearer of light & fire's rage,
        forger of armor which shines, Virgil tells us,

like sapphire clouds backlit by sun & the intricate
    shield Aeneas could not stop gazing upon, tracing,
        on its hammered bronze, the minutia of battle —

blood-wet briars, moon-glint of spears — & all
    the work of men, even if, after years of silence,
        you're summoned up again as war slogs on,

know this is floundering more than praise. This is a painter
    reduced to allegorizing Love & War, despite
        the khaki-teeming tents of Arras, a place before now

he knew only for the tapestries burned in the wake
    of the Bastille for the gold threads woven in,
        & how the Met housed one that survived,

with its warp & weft of wind-blown oaks, clustering
    ferns, Gabriel's tumbling, jade green sleeves
        & the ruby-crowned Virgin, interrupted from her book,

regarding the angel blankly, as if baffled by this
    unexpected task, just as Sargent, tongue-tied, wanders
        bomb-gouged streets, watching soldiers lounge

against whatever hasn't yet collapsed or the flood
    of light in a cathedral's ruin. Some days, in truth,
        he only half-seeks the muse, meandering instead

to a creek where the men bathe, doze, sun-dry
    their bodies of such blinding gleam he keeps their flesh
        empty on the page, affording them shape through

a fretwork of grass & cattail streaking chest & thigh,
    a shadow-scribbled lushness many worlds away
        from the wire-strewn fields, as if these watercolors

had been dashed out the summer before when he inhaled
    Florida's palmettos, tawny lagoons, the dappled
        mud-glistening alligator backs, when not bored

by yet-more hired portrait work & the white pleats
    of Rockefeller's pants. Gun-glint in a trench,
        lumbering convoys, a sugar factory's remains,

two Tommies filching sun-warmed cherries —
    for two months, he's been dabbling en plein air, lost
        in the sea of his commission, stymied by the 9 x 20

epic he needs to lure, as he put it, into your lace-like net.
    Castaway, crippled one, lord of all bright hissing steel,
        these words are not meant as invocation, unless

prayer means the way we limp towards form.
> *I have seen what I wanted*, Sargent writes at last,
>> & on site begins to sketch the line of gassed,

blindfolded men. Helmet straps, boots, a canteen
> tipped back, crease of each face-knotting cloth.
>> And eye-seared soldiers, shuffling beneath what will be

a pale-ochre sky & even now grouped on the page
> in tercet-like threes, even now spaced as orderly as
>> the lavish, binding mesh made by a god long dead.

To No One

Fucking bananas is how it'll be, your mother insisted,
grinning. *All the goddamn time.* Not that it matters now,
our small unmade, our might-have-been. You'll never know

the paltry wish I once held for you: to be content, aflame
with anything, & I swear
                         the abstract there was the point.
Except now I can never explain to you the empty distance

between idea & the toilet-soggy tail of a stuffed monkey
belonging to a kid no longer the invincible Stretchy Boy,
but only a boy, awake in terror, lips trembling, repeating

into my chest, *A green thing with teeth.* Once again,
here I am speaking to you
                          as I might the gods: unbelieving,
unable to stop. Although I'd like to tonight. I want

sleep more than this view of moon-slaked patio bricks
& remembering again
                     a paper cup filled with piss,
the dipped-in stick of plastic we preened over

in our robes, confusing the concrete with what seemed
indelible — that slow-appearing blue line. Bit of bedlam
we hoped to summon, you might have been another

bellowing goombah like your brother, beloved
& wondering at the impossible
                               elasticity of your arms,

which would be, of course, merely human arms merely

reaching for a tugboat, a chewed periwinkle crayon,
for the black-shelled snail
                         glistening unlikely
on asphalt during one afternoon's errand slog.

Van Gogh's First Sunday Sermon

I. *The setting sun casts a glory*

                      but this Sunday hour, it's not
the actual smack of Thames-blazing light, ivy bronzed
on gilt-edged elms, but brilliance hazed into allegory,
a hodgepodge of riffs on the Lord. It's the same all through
his pulpit-spouted words: ground of our heart, road from earth,
great storms not crow-swift & churning reddish wheat,
but ham-fisted into glosses on faith.

                                  Let us not forget things are not what they seem.

                   Not the frail aster or doorless peat shed,
the scroll of mist climbing from dew-drenched fields he describes
to Theo back home. Not a bonfire's flickering, snow-cast glint
or smears of carmine & malachite green that will become, in part,
in a life far removed from this short-lived now, stems of slender bulrush,
peach trees in bloom.

              I once saw a very beautiful painting:
it was a landscape at evening

                  but even this foothold of particulars —
fog-blue hills, heath of tawny leaves — turns to fill-in-the-gap doctrine
by the time he swerves to the pilgrim walking staff in hand. By then
the road, of course, is not a cart-rutted stretch weaving through
ditch grass & wind-mauled dunes, & the figure alone on the path
swells into nothing less than all of us, moving towards a mountain
that is not a mountain but a stand-in for grace to come

Our life

is a pilgrim's progress

                beneath specks of moon-dimmed stars,
blue-grey shadows of lemon trees, birch, reeling down a lane
in Arles, razor in hand. Where the scent of oleander lifts
to meet chestnut rot, what's left of lavender stalks, stale piss
at the brothel's backdoor where he offers half of his ear swaddled in cloth,
telling the girl, *Guard this object,* this one staggering crimsoned thing.

I am a stranger on earth

                he avows to the pews, though how different
to hear this phrase rustle through the work, through each garden shape
sketched in that last letter he sends. And even if words have become,
as he avows there, poor vessels for how he feels, he still names
in a postscript what he's made today: hazel tree, wicket, lilac hedge.

Protect me o God, for my bark is so small.

                Creed of grass, of leaf.
Pale green sky & a single figure beneath it, journeying nowhere at all.

II. *Let us cast out our net once more*

and for a while, let us not excerpt the long-ago, but allow
last week to make its claims too. Because isn't it too easy
to answer abstractions of faith with a garden's found grace,

his sequestered in-bloom scene testifying to flower, branch?
Couldn't I find my secular quick fix in any Van Gogh
thick-layered stroke, even his sunflower's ocher-flare

emblazing a MOMA wall clock, the faux-pearl heaven
of a *Starry Night* purse? Besides, isn't the distance
from that last sketch & the actual earth as long as the gap

from that pilgrim's illustrative walk & tramping in fact
a slushy, switchback path where scrub oaks quiver
with finches? By mountaintop, he meant the Lord's throne,

by black-inked diagonal slash, he means a blossom's magenta
splendor. Or, even more precise, he means stippled violet
on canvas, since this garden is a sketch of a painting

facsimiled in a book I hold. Tell me my faith in human touch
is different from what he pronounced to the pews. Tell me
one answer to the solitary figure of his sermon's non-road

is not just another drawing I happened to see, but a woman
I can't forget from a few days before, hysterical, wailing,
tearing through snow pack toward our car. The woman

ran towards us on Northpoint Road — a claim meaning,
as if it were possible, nothing else at all — & told us
through tears what happened: while watching

someone's daughter for the afternoon, she stepped into
a room for a moment & then the child was gone. For hours,
she'd been screaming her name into silence & the girl,

wearing a thin pink dress, couldn't last in the January cold.
Even if I tell you she'll soon be found — snot-smudged,
folded into the laundry room cupboard where she'd hidden

with detergent & pipes — that doesn't change how,
for a time, nothing else mattered, how everything
narrowed to this. While this stranger wept & fisted her hair,

my wife hunted for a phone & I stood in the road, holding my son,
who couldn't stop proclaiming the sound of crows & the color
of the woman's coat: *blue, blue, blue.*
Open Thou our eyes

that we may behold wondrous things. For what felt like a long time,
we stood in the snow-glare, half-blind, unsure what to do,
looking for any sign at all — a cast off shoe, footprint splay —

or even, somewhere, amen, the brilliant pink of the actual child.

Notes

Still Life with Burnt Lake
The concluding italicized lines are taken from Seymour Hacker's translation of Paul Cezanne's last letter. See *Paul Cezanne: Letters* (Da Capo Press, 1995).

Prelude for Musical Glasses
Melville's brief haunting story about the honey hunter concludes the "Cistern and Buckets" chapter of *Moby-Dick*: "Only one sweeter end can readily be recalled—the delicious death of an Ohio honey-hunter, who seeking honey in the crotch of a hollow tree, found such exceeding store of it, that leaning too far over, it sucked him in, so that he died embalmed. How many, think ye, have likewise fallen into Plato's honey head, and sweetly perished there?"

Elegy With Mistakes All Through It
Edward A. Berlin's *King of Ragtime: Scott Joplin and His Era* (Oxford University Press, 2016) provided some of the details regarding Joplin's life in this elegy for William Appling, a beloved, passionate, iconoclastic, and forever inspiring teacher.

Poem in which Billie Holiday Is Barely Heard
In Donald Clarke's *Billie Holiday: Wishing on the Moon* (Da Capo Press, 2002), Holiday's initial confusion after taking the Carnegie Hall stage is described in devastating detail. "What am I supposed to be singing?" she cried out to pianist Memry Midget while the band circled back to the song's introduction yet again.

Sargent Adrift at the Trenches
The Sargent painting described in this poem is *Gassed*, now in London's Imperial War Museum. For details of the painter's time on the Western Front, I'm indebted to Charles Merrill Mount's *John Singer Sargent: A Biography* (Cresset Press, 1957).

Van Gogh's First Sunday Sermon
Although Van Gogh's fall from the church might, in retrospect, be viewed as inevitable ("I prefer painting people's eyes to cathedrals," he would later write in a letter to his brother Theo), he pursued a life of divinity with characteristic fervor, and his break from the ministry was ultimately initiated by Dutch authorities who judged his acts of charity as needlessly excessive. For the quoted lines from his sermon, I relied on the Bullfinch Press edition of *The Complete Letters of Vincent Van Gogh* (2000).

Acknowledgments

Some of these poems, sometimes in different versions, previously appeared in the following publications:

AGNI
"Bessie Smith's Last Recorded Song," "Elegy with Mistakes All Through It," "Perhaps We Are What We Want to Remember," "Rapture & the Big Bam," "Two Songs About the Work of Hands," and "Van Gogh's First Sunday Sermon"

American Poetry Review
"Exit, Pursued by a Bear"

Gettysburg Review
"Prelude for Musical Glasses"

Harvard Review
"Still Life with Burnt Lake"

Kenyon Review
"Poem in which Billie Holiday Is Barely Heard"

Literary Imagination
"To No One"

Ninth Letter
"How to Paint the Sea"

Post Road
"Sargent Adrift at the Trenches"

Virginia Quarterly Review
"Motel Makeshift Lullaby"

Enormous gratitude is due to Lia Purpura, for selecting these poems as judge of the Snowbound contest. To Jeffrey Levine and all of the excellent folks at Tupelo, especially Jim Schley for his stellar editorial work. To the editors of the journals in which these pieces previously appeared, with a special thanks to Sven Birkerts and Bill Pierce at *AGNI*, who first hauled on board many of these poems. To Kathy Graber, Dana Levin, Tom Sleigh, and David Wojahn, for their years of guidance, encouragement, and shrewd feedback on my work. To my parents, who fanned the flames early on, and who never waver in their support. To Cyrus and Oliver, my beloved bellowing boys. And above all and always to Ligia Bouton, my first reader, my absolute.

Matt Donovan is the author of a previous book of poems, *Vellum* (Mariner Books, 2007), and a collection of essays, *A Cloud of Unusual Size and Shape: Meditations on Ruin and Redemption* (Trinity University Press, 2016). He is the recipient of a Rome Prize in Literature, a Whiting Writer's Award, a Pushcart Prize, a National Endowment for the Arts fellowship, and the Larry Levis Reading Prize from Virginia Commonwealth University. He teaches at Santa Fe University of Art and Design and is currently collaborating on a chamber opera entitled *Inheritance*, about the life and legends of firearms heiress Sarah Winchester.

www.ingramcontent.com/pod-product-compliance
Lightning Source LLC
Chambersburg PA
CBHW041959080526

44588CB00021B/2812